Trains

by Julie Murray

ABDO
TRANSPORTATION
Kids

Visit us at www.abdopublishing.com

Published by Abdo Kids, a division of ABDO, PO Box 398166, Minneapolis, Minnesota 55439.

Printed in the United States of America, North Mankato, Minnesota.

032014

092014

 PRINTED ON RECYCLED PAPER

Photo Credits: Shutterstock, Thinkstock, © User:JIP/Wikimedia Commons/CC-BY-SA-3.0 p.13

Production Contributors: Teddy Borth, Jennie Forsberg, Grace Hansen

Design Contributors: Dorothy Toth, Laura Rask

Library of Congress Control Number: 2013953015

Cataloging-in-Publication Data

Murray, Julie.

Trains / Julie Murray.

  p. cm. -- (Transportation)

ISBN 978-1-62970-082-3 (lib. bdg.)

Includes bibliographical references and index.

1. Trains--Juvenile literature. I. Title.

625.1--dc23

     2013953015

Table of Contents

Trains

Whoo! Whoo! The train whistle blows. The train moves along the tracks.

4

5

Trains carry people and **goods** from one place to another.

Parts of a Train

The front of the train is called the **locomotive**. It holds the engine and pulls the train cars.

9

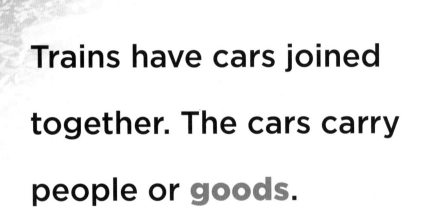

Trains have cars joined together. The cars carry people or **goods**.

Different Kinds of Trains

Passenger trains carry people. You can eat and sleep on some trains.

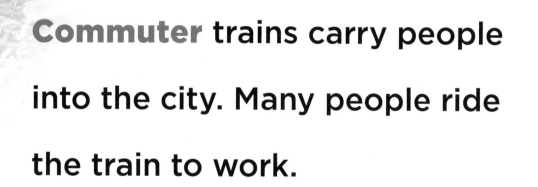

Commuter trains carry people into the city. Many people ride the train to work.

14

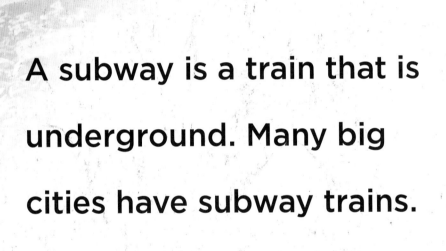

A subway is a train that is underground. Many big cities have subway trains.

The UK's

via C Airport

17

Freight trains carry **goods**.
They carry things like coal
and grain.

18

19

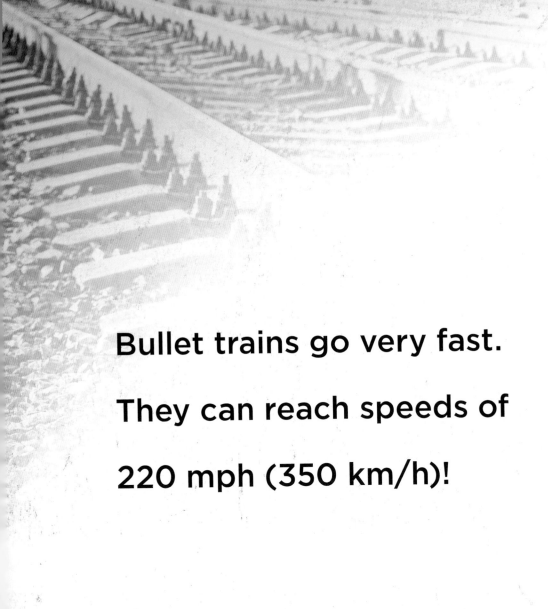

Bullet trains go very fast.

They can reach speeds of

220 mph (350 km/h)!

21

More Facts

- Grand Central station in New York has the most platforms of any train station in the world.

- In the United States, trains are mostly used to transport **goods**.

- **Freight** trains in the United States average about 1.2 miles (2,000 m) in length, spanning 70 cars carrying 3,000 tons (2,721,550 kg).

- Horses pulled the first trains.

Glossary

commuter – a train that carries passengers regularly from one place to another.

freight – a train that carries goods or cargo.

goods – merchandise when transported.

locomotive – an engine used for pulling or pushing a train or individual railroad cars.

passenger – a train that carries passengers. Passengers are people who want to go from one place to another.

Index

abdokids.com

Use this code to log on to abdokids.com and access crafts, games, videos and more!

Abdo Kids Code:
TTK0823